Contents

Introduction

'I don't know much about it.'
'I haven't really thought about it.'

We live in a complicated world, and it's full of people telling us what to think. In the papers, on TV and radio we find people trying to get us on their side. It's hard to get the information you need to make up your **own** mind. So many things are a matter of opinion.

This book is one of a series that aims to help you to work out what you think about some of the topics that are in the news these days. We've tried to make the books easy to read so that you can sort out the facts for yourself and decide which points of view you think are important. We don't expect you to agree with everything you read here, but we hope it will start you thinking.

You can read this book by yourself but you might also like to talk to other people about some of the ideas you find here, or do something to find out more about the topic for yourself. This is easier if you're in touch with a group of other readers—in an adult education centre or a college, for instance. Then you can work out your opinions and find out more together. There

A MATTER OF OPINION

Whose Life?

Miriam Sampson

JOHN MURRAY

A MATTER OF OPINION

Series Editor Miriam Sampson

Living with Computers Irene and Ronald Cretchley

What about Women? Juliet McCaffery

A Good Buy Pamela Rayson

Whose Life? Miriam Sampson

First published 1985
by John Murray (Publishers) Ltd
50 Albemarle Street
London W1X 4BD

Typeset by Fakenham Photosetting Ltd
Fakenham, Norfolk
Printed in Great Britain by
Martin's of Berwick

British Library Cataloguing in Publication Data

Sampson, Miriam
Whose life?—(A Matter of opinion)
1. Readers for new literates
I. Title II. Series
428.6'2 PE1126.A4

ISBN 0-7195-4005-4

are some ideas in the book about how you might do this.

Whose Life? looks at life and death choices that are being made today. Scientists and doctors are finding out more every day about how life begins. New ways of treating sick people are being discovered all the time. This book looks in particular at abortion, mercy-killing and the future for handicapped babies. When you've read it, keep your eyes open for news and views about other life and death choices. Some examples might be 'test-tube' babies and experiments on human embryos; women acting as 'surrogate mothers' for someone else's baby; or arguments about who should be able to have expensive treatment to keep them alive.

We hope that you'll enjoy reading this book and that it will help you to work out what **your** opinions are.

A modern family

1

Looking at life

Most of us get on with the business of living without thinking very much about how our lives begin and end, but every so often something happens which makes us think about matters of life and death.

Perhaps there's a new baby in the family and we're struck by the miracle of life. Maybe a relative has an incurable disease, and we know she's going to die. Perhaps a friend is injured in an accident, and he's seriously handicapped as a result.

These sorts of events bring us up against the facts of life and death. They can also force us to think about the choices we have today in matters of life and death.

Choices about birth

Today most people plan their families. They decide how many children they want and they choose a method of birth control to make sure they don't have more.

If a woman finds she's pregnant when she doesn't want a baby, she may be offered an abortion. For every 100 babies born in Britain in 1982, over 20 were aborted. But many people believe abortion is wrong because a baby's life is involved.

Choices about death

Some people die suddenly. Others linger on. Many people fear that they might be kept alive when they're unable to do any of the things that make life worth living for them. They want to be able to choose when to die.

Should we be able to ask our doctors to end our lives when we feel we've had enough? Or is it always wrong to take someone's life?

Choices about handicap

Some people are born handicapped. What sorts of lives will they lead? Some doctors believe that badly handicapped babies should not be treated. They should be allowed to die. Their lives wouldn't be worth living.

Should doctors be able to decide who will live and who will die? When it's a baby's life, how much say should the parents have?

A 100 years ago we wouldn't have had to ask these questions. Abortion was very dangerous. Many illnesses couldn't be treated. Most handicapped babies—and many normal babies too—died soon after birth. We live longer than our great grandparents, and we're healthier. But new treatments have brought new problems. Difficult decisions have to be made.

Is it morbid to think about these life and death decisions? Many of us will have to face one of these problems at some time in our lives. Perhaps you have already. It can be helpful to work out what we think before we have to decide for ourselves.

2

A right to live?

'In these days, when everyone is anxious for women to have the right to be independent, they should have the right to decide what happens to their bodies. Women **do** want abortion...'

Jo Richardson MP, *Woman's Own*, June 1983

'No woman has the right to kill. Women don't really want abortions ... To go through an abortion is the saddest thing and only a woman who has, can tell you.'

Nuala Scarisbrick, Hon. Administrator of Life, *Woman's Own*, June 1983

Abortion removes the foetus (unborn baby) from its mother's womb before it is able to survive in the world outside.

When we think about abortion we need to work out our opinions on points like these:

- Should women have the right to choose an abortion?
- What are the alternatives to abortion for a woman who doesn't want the baby she's expecting?

- What part should doctors play in decisions about abortion?
- Does the present law on abortion get the balance right or does it need to be changed?

The information in the next two chapters may help you to work out what you think.

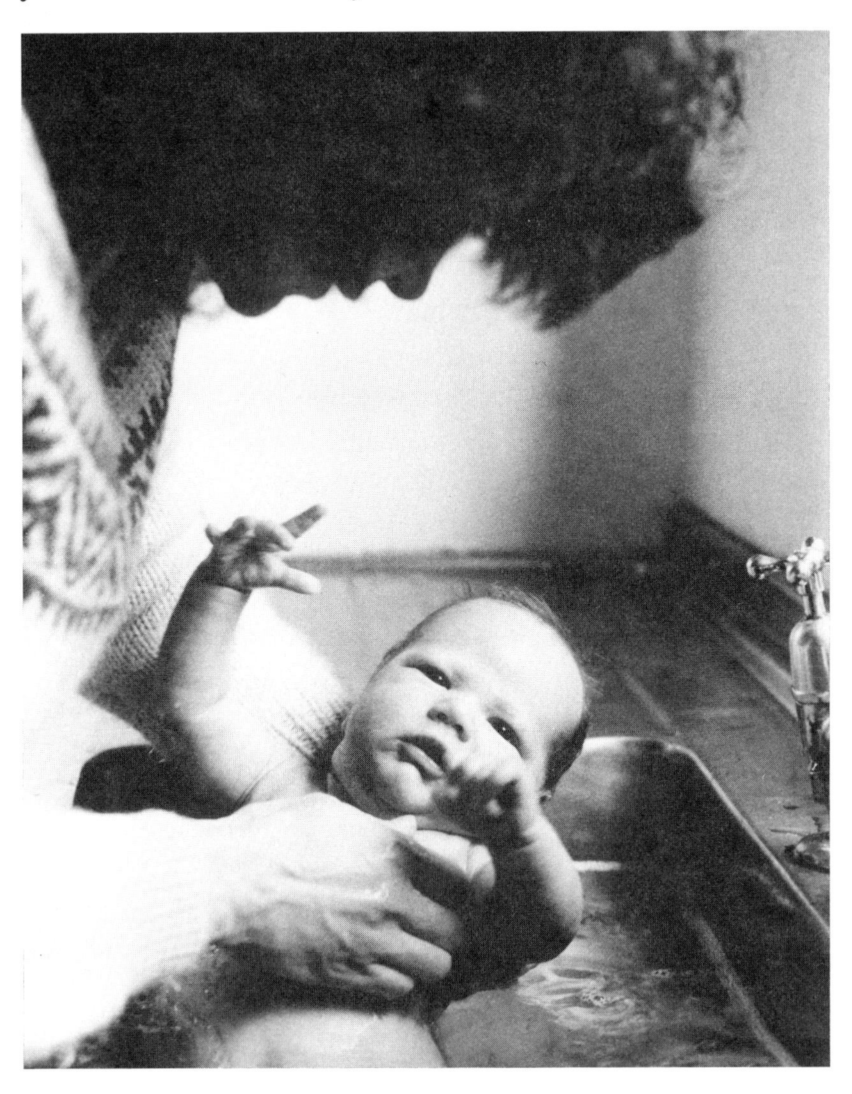

3

A happy event?

'Congratulations on the happy event.' That's what the greetings cards say when a new baby's born. But when a woman first finds out she's expecting a baby it isn't always such good news. Of course, many women are thrilled to be pregnant, but for others there can be difficulties.

Single and pregnant?—'What will my boyfriend do? Will he stand by me? Could I bring up a child on my own?'

Under pressure?—'My husband's out of work. We can't afford another child.'

Would an abortion be the answer to the problems these women face? How will they decide?

In the past

Until 1967, abortion was illegal in Britain except in cases where the mother's life was in danger.

Some women had abortions in hospitals and clinics if they could prove that having a baby would ruin their

health. Private clinics were expensive. Poor women might go to a 'back-street' abortionist. This was illegal and could also be dangerous. Many women became ill, and some died, as a result of infection following back-street abortions.

Sally had an illegal abortion when she was 19. This was shortly before she became engaged to the man who's now her husband. It seemed to be the only thing to do at the time, though Sally later felt he pushed her into it. Then when she wanted a child she had problems with her pregnancy and she lost her baby. Since then she's been unable to conceive.

Sally has tried to adopt a baby, but now that the law on abortion has changed there are few babies available. How does Sally feel now?

> 'One thing for sure is that I've changed my mind about abortion. I feel I can't have children and that because of the abortion laws I can't even adopt one.'

Before the law was changed in 1967, a few women did have abortions free in National Health Service (NHS) hospitals. Girls under the age of 16 and women with large families were most likely to get free abortions.

Abortion today

In 1967, Parliament passed a new Act to make abortion legal in Britain under certain conditions. Two doctors have to sign a certificate giving the reasons for the abortion. The pregnant woman can ask for an abortion but the doctors have to agree that her case comes within the law.

What does the law say? Abortions can legally be carried out in this country for four reasons. The pregnancy must present:

- a risk to the life of the pregnant woman, or
- a risk of injury to her physical or mental health, or
- a risk of injury to the physical or mental health of her existing children, or

- a substantial risk that if the child was born it would be seriously handicapped, physically or mentally.

What does all this mean? Who can have an abortion?

It really depends on what the doctors think. Many doctors would have no doubts. Four out of every five abortions carried out in Britain are done under the 'social clause'—'risk of injury to the physical or mental health of the pregnant woman'. This clause has been used to allow abortions for women who have housing problems, whose jobs are at risk, and so on.

The number of abortions went up sharply after the 1967 Act was passed. But the number carried out because the mother's life is at risk has gone down. With good pregnancy care very few mothers' lives are at risk from pregnancy in Britain today.

In 1981, 162,454 abortions were carried out in England and Wales.

The figures below show the main reasons given for these abortions. Sometimes more than one reason was given.

Reason stated on form	Number of times this reason was mentioned
1 Risk to mother's life	787
2 Risk of injury to her health	158,499
3 Risk to her children's health	20,707
4 Risk of handicapped baby	2,052

Not all these abortions were carried out under the NHS. Private clinics and 'pregnancy advisory services', which are registered charities, can also do them. Women going to any of these clinics will have to pay. In 1983, the operation cost at least £100 at one of the cheaper clinics. An abortion carried out after the first 20 weeks of pregnancy would cost more than £250.

A difficult decision?

Some women find the decision to have an abortion is easy to make. That was how **Maggy** felt:

> 'I knew that I was pregnant before the doctor told me ... At the time I was living with my boyfriend ... a child would have drastically altered our lives. I found him supportive but his occasional remarks such as "Wouldn't it be nice to have a baby?" worried me...
> The abortion was quick, very straightforward and relatively painless...
> I went back to work 2 days later feeling relieved it was all over, but the heavy bleeding lasted for over 2 weeks and that kept reminding me.'

Some women, like **Sally**, feel they have no choice at the time but end up regretting it. Others start out feeling sure they want an abortion but then change their minds.

In 1974, a government report suggested that all

women seeking an abortion should receive 'counselling' beforehand. That's an opportunity to talk to someone about everything that's involved, to make sure the woman knows what she's doing and won't regret it. But that doesn't always happen. Some women have abortions and then decide that they really do want a baby, so they are pregnant again a few months later.

A woman's issue?

Is abortion just a woman's issue or is it something that concerns all of us? When a woman is faced with an unplanned pregnancy and the possibility of abortion, she may feel very alone. But, whatever she decides, other people are involved too—the man in her life and her doctor, for a start. Doctors who are asked to carry out abortions have to take the law into account, and that law was drawn up by lawyers and passed by Members of Parliament. Ordinary people elected the MPs and many voters have strong opinions about it.

So this issue concerns us all. And we shouldn't forget the person for whom it's a matter of life and death—the unborn baby.

4

Whose life is it?

Don't know—don't care?

From time to time abortion hits the headlines. One of these times was 1979, when John Corrie MP was trying to tighten up the 1967 Abortion Act. There was a lot of argument, both inside Parliament and outside. The BBC used a Gallup Poll to collect people's views. (You'll find some of the results on page 27.) Sooner or later the matter is bound to come up in Parliament again and we could all have a chance to make our views known. It's worth thinking about what's involved before that time comes.

Get the facts

The chart on pages 20 and 21 shows what's happening to the pregnant woman and her unborn baby during the first 28 weeks of pregnancy, when it's legal to carry out an abortion. Most of the baby's growth takes place during the first 20 weeks. Most of the risks to the mother's health occur after that.

The chart also lists the methods of abortion that can be used at each stage of pregnancy.

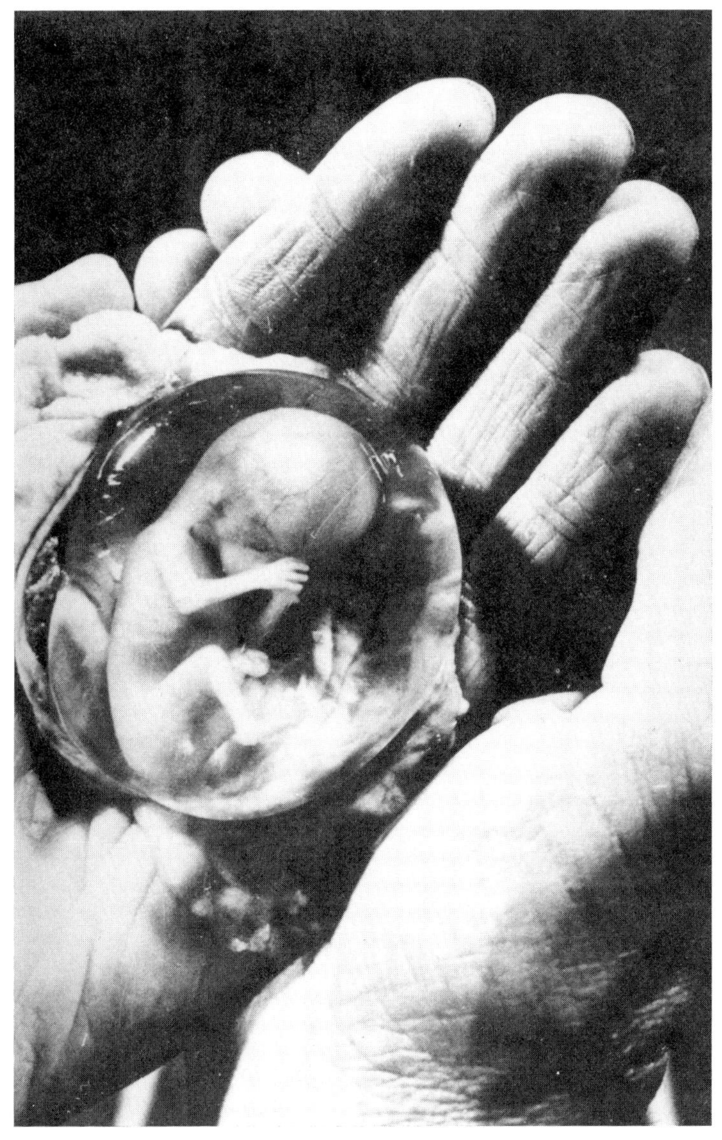

A foetus aborted at 10 weeks. The head, hands and feet can be seen clearly

Stage of pregnancy	**What's happening to the pregnant woman?**	**What's happening to the growing baby?**	**Method of abortion used**
6 weeks	Period 2 weeks late. Suspects she's pregnant and test may give a positive result	Body is $\frac{1}{4}$ inch long. Has head, trunk, arm buds. Heart is beating	Vacuum aspiration. Tube put into the neck of the womb. Foetus sucked out into a jar. (Torn apart in the process)
9 weeks	Has missed second period. May have 'morning sickness' and feel ill and tired	Still less than 1 inch long, but has eyes, ears, nose, lips, tongue. First teeth already in the gums. Hands have fingers and thumbs	Vacuum aspiration or 'D and C'. Neck of womb stretched open. Contents of womb—including foetus—scraped out
12 weeks	Pregnancy still does not show. May still feel ill	Moves in response to touch on most parts of the body. Girls and boys look different	Vacuum aspiration now difficult

Stage of pregnancy	What's happening to the pregnant woman?	What's happening to the growing baby?	Method of abortion used
18 weeks	'Morning sickness' usually over. Gaining weight now and probably feeling well. Clothes no longer fit—pregnancy shows. May have felt baby moving	8–10 inches long. Weighs about 6 ounces. Test done on 'waters' surrounding baby may show up abnormalities	Labour induced by injection of salt solution or hormone called prostaglandin. Foetus absorbs salt—skin is burnt off and baby is born dead
20 weeks	HALFWAY POINT IN NORMAL PREGNANCY		
24 weeks	Feels baby moving strongly	Heartbeat can be heard through stethoscope. Moves a lot. Can hear loud noises in outside world, e.g. door slamming. If born prematurely may now survive with special care	Same methods as at 18 weeks, or hysterotomy—like a Caesarian birth. Some nurses have claimed babies have been born alive after these late operations

What are the risks to the woman?

Any operation carries some risk and an abortion is no exception. Early abortions, in the first 8 weeks of pregnancy, are usually trouble free. Abortion becomes more difficult after the eighth week. Abortion in later pregnancy may cause a lot more complications.

Some problems don't show up until the woman is pregnant again. Since the neck of the womb is stretched in an abortion there's a risk of miscarriage in another pregnancy. Women who have had abortions are four times more likely to lose a later baby than other women. Even early abortions carry this risk.

If infection sets in after an abortion it can be dangerous. It can cause sterility, or even death. Infection is most likely after 'back-street' abortions done in dirty conditions. Many people hoped these would stop when abortion was legalised. Yet today some women still end up in hospital with complications after back-street abortions.

Is it dangerous to delay?

Some women have to wait if they want an abortion on the NHS. These are the delays that one woman met.

- When she first saw her doctor she was told it was too early for a pregnancy test. She should come back in a month.
- It took 10 days for the result of her pregnancy test to come through.

- She was referred to the hospital. She had to wait 3 weeks for an appointment because the consultant was on holiday.
- After she saw the consultant she had to wait for the operation because he went away again.
- In the end she went to a private clinic when she was 21 weeks pregnant.

Would these problems be solved if more early abortions could be done in day-care clinics where a simple operation is done under a local anaesthetic? Or could this lead to more women opting to have abortions before they've thought things through, and regretting it later?

Pressures for change

At the moment there are several groups in Britain campaigning for changes to the Abortion Act.

The groups on one side want to make abortion easier to obtain. Their slogan is 'A Woman's Right to Choose'.

The groups on the other side want to make abortions more difficult to obtain. Their slogan is 'A Right to Life'.

Here are some of the points made by the two sides. Do they help you to decide what you think should happen?

A woman's right to choose	A right to life
Legal abortions carried out early in pregnancy are safe and easy. Women should be able to choose for themselves. If they didn't have to get permission for an abortion from a doctor, delays could be cut down and abortions carried out more safely.	Abortion kills unborn children who have a right to life. The baby is a person right from conception. It depends on its mother's body, but it's not just part of it. Its life should be protected by law because abortion is murder.
It's a woman's right to choose what happens to her body. The foetus is part of her body. It has no life of its own before it's born.	Abortion can be dangerous for women. An abortion can harm a woman's health, mentally as well as physically. An abortion won't solve a woman's problems—it could add to them.

Wanted or unwanted?

There's one more argument that we need to think about. One side says that every child should be a wanted child, and easier abortion would help. The other side claims that an unwelcome pregnancy need not result in an unloved child.

Every child a wanted child (A right to choose)

A woman should be able to choose how many children to have and when to have them. If birth control fails, an abortion may avoid bringing an unwanted child into the world.

A new baby's arrival can stretch the family budget so much that the other children suffer. Unwanted children may also become 'battered babies'. In the late 1970s, over 100,000 children in Britain were in children's homes or foster homes because their own parents couldn't take care of them properly. It's wise for a woman to choose to end her pregnancy if she knows she couldn't give her child proper care.

> 'What women want is a real choice between having a safe, legal abortion if they don't want children and having an adequate standard of living so that they can bring up the children they do want with dignity.'
>
> 'Where we Stand'—National Abortion Campaign

An unwelcome pregnancy need not result in an unloved child (A right to life)

It's quite usual for a woman in the early weeks of pregnancy to have mixed feelings about having a baby. She may feel tired and sick, and think she could never cope with the demands a baby will make. If the pregnancy wasn't planned she may be in a state of shock. It takes time to get used to the idea of having a child.

There is help available. The Life organisation, as well as campaigning against abortion, aims 'to give free, practical help to any woman facing a difficult pregnancy and to support her as far as possible during and after pregnancy'. In 1982, Life had 39,000 calls from women wanting pregnancy tests,

counselling and practical help during pregnancy. It provided accommodation for several hundred pregnant women in 62 'Life houses' throughout Britain.
Life can also provide baby clothes and equipment and give friendship and support both during pregnancy and after the birth.

Some single women decide to have their babies adopted. This may be hard, but they'll know that their child is living in a family where he or she is wanted and will be given loving care.

> 'The right response to the problem pregnancy is to give practical help—not to reject, not to destroy.'
>
> Life

What's your verdict?

The BBC Gallup Poll of 1979 asked people for their views on abortion. This is what they said about the abortion laws.

The present laws on abortion	Men	Women	All
(a) are satisfactory	24%	27%	26%
(b) should be altered to make abortion easier to obtain	22%	16%	19%
(c) should be altered to make abortion more difficult to obtain	32%	43%	38%
(d) don't know	22%	14%	18%

Did you notice that more men than women wanted abortion to be easier to obtain, but more women than men wanted it to be more difficult. What do you make of this result? How would **you** reply?

Life before birth?

Is abortion just another form of birth control? Or is it murder? How important is life before birth?

Today people are asking questions about the rights and wrongs of producing 'test-tube babies', because the unwanted embryos are thrown away after one has successfully settled in the womb. They are also worried about the idea that human embryos can be used for research, though some people say this could help us find out more about serious diseases.

If we are concerned about the rights of tiny embryos, how do we feel about the abortions that have been carried out since 1967 up to the twenty-eighth week of pregnancy, when a baby is fully formed? Some people want even this time limit abolished to allow abortions right up to birth. So where should we draw the line on abortion? Do you see it as a matter of life and death?

5

A right to die?

'Surely it is time to ask why thousands of dying, incurable and senile persons are being kept alive … who unmistakably want to die.'

Professor O. R. Russell, *New York Times*, 1972

'A few days before I came here the pain got so bad that I was afraid I would die. By the time I got here I was afraid I wouldn't. But now I'm here, I'm glad I didn't.'

Mr R., a patient in a London hospice

Now that abortion is legal, will mercy-killing (euthanasia) be legalised too? When we think about the end of life we need to work out our opinions on points like these:

- Should a doctor always try to keep his patients alive as long as possible, even if the treatment makes them feel worse?
- If someone is so ill that he feels his life's no longer worth living, should he be able to ask his doctor to end it for him?

- Are there other ways, apart from euthanasia, to help people end their lives in comfort?
- Should the law be changed to legalise euthanasia?

The information in the next two chapters may help you to work out what you think.

6

We can't live for ever

Our bodies aren't made to last for ever. At the age of 25 most of us don't think twice about walking upstairs. By the age of 75 we'll probably want to avoid stairs if we can. Although doctors can now do operations to renew a hip or knee joint, transplant kidneys or put pacemakers in the heart, they can't keep us alive for ever. In the end we must all die, if only of old age.

Some deaths are sudden. A heart attack can strike with little or no warning. Other diseases slowly cause death. Many people have a special fear of cancer for this reason. In Britain today one person in five dies of cancer, but many more fear that they may.

About two-thirds of us will die in hospital, in the care of doctors and nurses. Yet doctors and nurses often keep off the subject of death just as much as the rest of us. They've been trained to save life and to treat disease. If all their skill fails to bring their patient back to health and they have to admit he's dying, they may not know how to cope.

Some of us—like this lady celebrating her eightieth birthday—enjoy good health in old age. But what happens when our health breaks down?

Should he know he's dying?

Sometimes a doctor won't tell his patient that he's dying. He leaves it to the relatives. If they try to avoid the subject, the dying person is left wondering what's going on. Perhaps he's already guessed that he's not going to get better, but he doesn't want to upset his family by talking about death. So everyone goes on pretending.

Some people don't want to face up to death. Mr H., who was very ill, was moved from hospital to a hospice, which gives special care to people who are dying. He made it clear to the doctor that he didn't want to talk about death: 'As far as I know I've been sent here for convalescence. That's as far as I know.'

Another person may be ready to die. The same doctor reports, 'Mr D. wondered if he would reach his next birthday, which was 3 weeks away. "Yes," I said, "but not the next one." He smiled and said, "Good, I don't want to."'

If you were in this position, would you want to know you were dying, or not? Do you think it's better to talk about it, or to keep quiet?

How should we deal with death?

When someone has an illness that isn't responding to treatment and it's clear he's going to die, what's the best thing to do? There are really three choices.

- Try everything to keep him alive as long as possible. This is often done in hospitals.
- Let him decide when he's had enough and choose his own time to die. Arrange for someone to end his life for him, before the disease kills him. This is known as euthanasia, or mercy-killing. At the moment it's illegal.

- Stop trying to cure the disease but try to stop any pain so that he can live as happily as possible until death comes. This is done in hospices.

Let's look at these choices in turn.

1 Treatment until the end

Mrs Arnold was in her sixties when she was found to have lung cancer. Treatment wasn't successful and in September she went into hospital for the last time. She died at the end of October.

For the last month of her life Mrs Arnold was fed liquids through a tube pushed up her nose. She tried to take the tube away. After this her hand was strapped down to stop her trying again.

After Mrs Arnold died her husband went to court. He wanted the judge to make it clear that patients have the right to refuse treatment they don't want. Mr Arnold said, 'I do feel that without the tube she would have been a lot happier and not suffered so. My wife was fighting against it. So they bound her left hand and kept it bound all day. That's how she died. It was a terrible experience, as I was completely helpless.'

Cases like this should never happen because every patient **does** have the right to refuse treatment. All the same, it can be difficult for the dying person or a close relative to refuse if the doctors insist that the treatment must go on. The fear of dying like this may make people feel that the only way to 'die with dignity' is to choose their own time to die.

Of course it's right to do everything possible to keep someone alive after an accident, or during an illness,

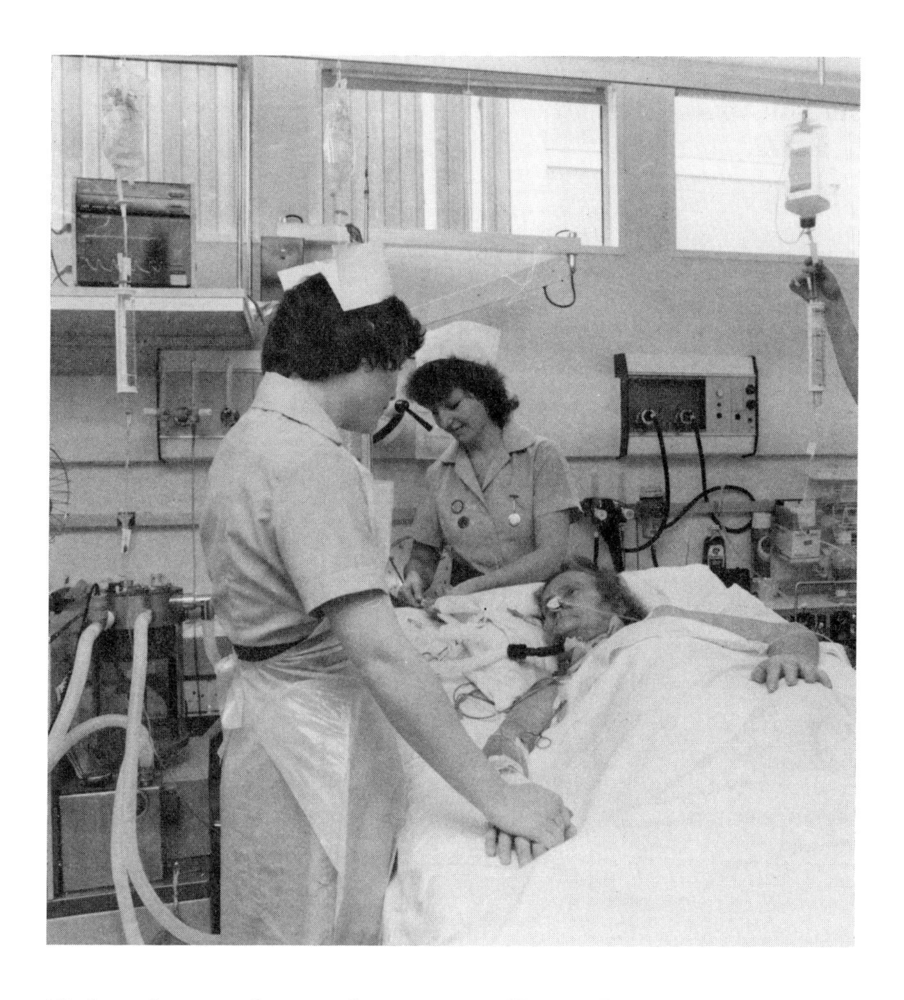

if there's any hope of recovery. But what should be done when there's no hope at all?

When someone is dying all sorts of things **can** be done. More operations or blood transfusions may keep the patient going for a few more weeks. He can be fed through a tube. Perhaps his heart can be kept beating and his breathing kept going with the help of a machine. But is this always the best thing to do? Can the effect of treatment like this be worse than the effects of the disease? It may only add to the dying person's pain and suffering.

2 Mercy-killing

In 1975, Jean died. She was only 42 but she had cancer. After her death her husband, Derek, wrote a book about Jean. It begins like this:

> 'As I placed the breakfast tray at my wife's bedside she looked across at me and asked, "Is this the day?"
> "Yes, my darling, it is," I replied. I had known for some time now.
> "All right," she declared, "I shall die at one o'clock. That's good. I'm glad it's been decided."'

That day was Easter Saturday 1975. Jean and Derek talked till it was almost one o'clock. Then Derek went to the kitchen to make some coffee. Into one mug he put a mixture of pain-killers and sleeping tablets which he knew would kill Jean. He gave her the mug. Derek's story goes on:

> '"Is this it?" she asked.
> She knew what it contained. We gave one another a last embrace while we said farewell. She gulped the coffee, set down the mug on the bedside table barely in time before she began to pass out, murmuring, "Good-bye, darling."
> She fell into a deep sleep, breathing heavily. I watched over her until 50 minutes later her breathing stopped.'

'Jean's way'

Jean had had several operations and other treatments to try to cure her cancer between 1972 and 1974. They didn't succeed. In August 1974, she spoke to Derek about the way she wanted to die:

> 'I want you to do something for me so that if I decide I want to die I can do it on my own terms and exactly when I choose. I shall have a good idea when I've had enough of the pain. So I want you to promise me that when I ask you if this is the right time to kill myself you will give me an honest answer one way or another and we must understand, both you and I, that I'll do it right at that very moment. You won't question my right and you will give me the means to do it.'

Derek admired Jean's strength of mind and he agreed to help her.

Jean had seen her mother die of cancer in great pain and she didn't want to go the same way. She wanted to die at home, with her husband, while she still knew what she was doing. Derek helped her as he'd promised. A doctor friend gave him some drugs. When Jean took them in her coffee on Easter Saturday 1975 she died at the time she had chosen.

The law on mercy-killing

Derek broke the law when he gave Jean that fatal dose. Suicide is no longer a crime, but it's still against the law to help someone to kill herself. He could have been sent to prison for up to 14 years.

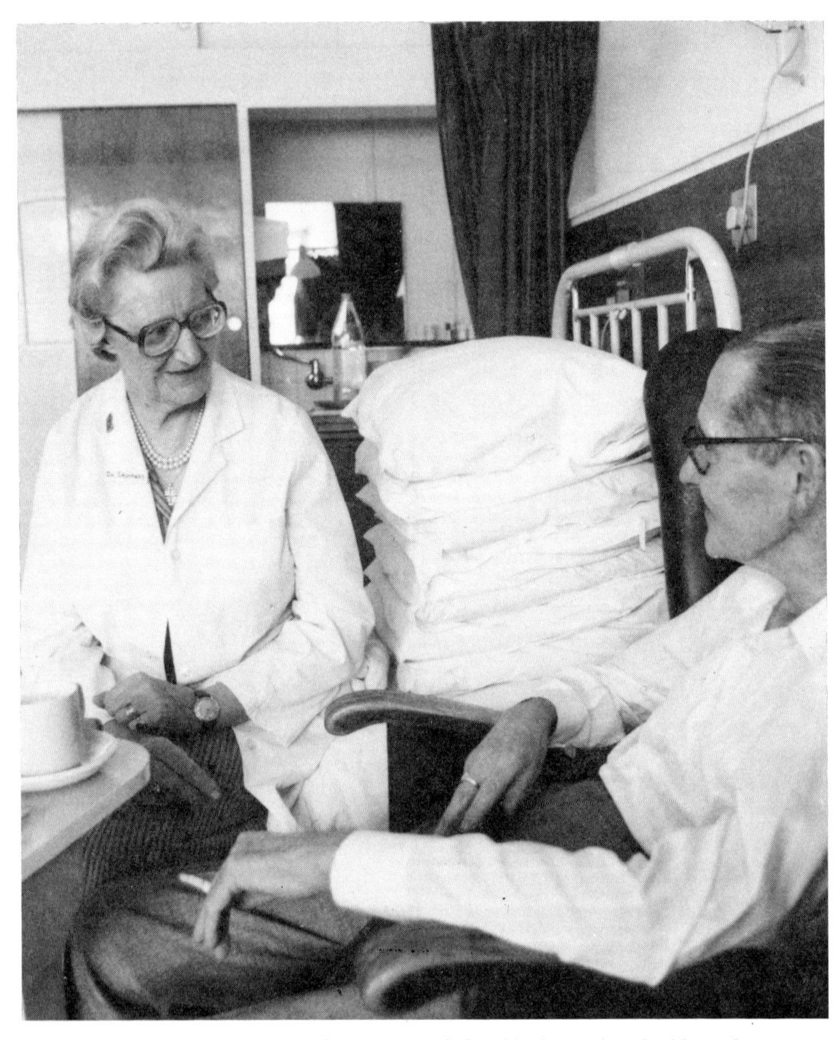

Dame Cicely Saunders, founder of St Christopher's Hospice, London, relaxing with one of her patients

About 10 cases of mercy-killing came before the English courts between 1978 and 1980 but none of the people charged went to prison. Since 1980, some people have been sent to prison for assisting people who asked for help to commit suicide.

3 Not cure—but care

Is mercy-killing the only alternative to a painful death? Many people don't think so. In recent years the hospice movement has been trying to work out new ways to care for people who are dying. In hospices the doctors aim to stop their patients' pain and to help them to live a worthwhile life right to the end.

Doctors and nurses in hospices aren't trying to **cure** disease; they are trying to **care** for their patients. This means caring about a person's feelings as well as his body. It means helping him to do the things he wants to do before he dies.

Here's one example. Mrs N. and her family were cared for by the staff of a hospice.

> 'This lady in her forties had come from the West Indies with four of her older children so that they could be well educated ... After a few years she was found to have breast cancer.'

Mrs N. had her breast removed but this operation didn't stop the cancer spreading. When she went into the hospice the doctor found out that she would love to see her younger children in Grenada but didn't suppose she ever would now.

The doctors treated Mrs N.'s pain and then started to find out if she might be able to fly home to Grenada. They arranged for one of Mrs N.'s sons to travel with her. Another son and her daughter raised most of the money.

It wasn't all plain sailing. First they had to persuade the customs men to let Mrs N. take two large bottles of heroin mixture with her. She wasn't smuggling drugs. She needed heroin as a pain-killer. Next they needed a fork-lift to get her wheelchair onto the plane. Then her son got lost in the airport and delayed the flight. At last they were off.

The doctor wrote, 'We received a triumphant letter from Grenada some weeks later. She had pain again but obviously considered it unimportant. A fortnight later she died, just 3 days after seeing her second daughter married in Grenada.'

Most patients in hospices don't fly half way round the world like Mrs N., but everything possible is done to keep them free from pain. The hospice staff try to help relatives to cope with death too. In many cases they can arrange for the patients to live comfortably at home until death comes, by sending specially trained staff to visit them at home and make sure all is well. Many people prefer this to dying in hospital.

'A totally different experience'

Sheila Hancock, the actress, has written about the deaths of her mother and her first husband. Both of them died of cancer. Sheila looked after her mother at home for as long as she could, but she wasn't a trained nurse and she didn't get much help from anyone else.

> 'I was often left in the middle of the night with my mother in absolute agony, not knowing where to turn.'

In the end her mother went into hospital, and died there. It was a very distressing experience for Sheila.

One month later her husband's cancer was diagnosed. This time the staff of a hospice gave support day and night so that he could stay at home right to the end. Sheila wrote:

> 'For me and my husband their method was 100% successful. It was a totally different experience from that with my mother...
> My husband and I went to the theatre 2 days before he died, because his drugs were dosed in such a way that he never became a vegetable, and his life, even though he was consumed with disease at the end, was always worth living.'

Is it possible that this type of care for people nearing death could solve the problems that push people towards mercy-killing?

7

A time to die?

A good death

Can death be good? The word 'euthanasia' comes from a Greek word meaning a good death. But it has come to mean something different today. Now it's used to mean death by someone's choice. Voluntary euthanasia is death chosen by the person himself.

Suicide is no longer a crime but it's still illegal to help someone to kill himself. Any doctor who gave his patient a fatal drug could be brought to trial even if he could prove that his patient had asked him to do it. Should the law be changed?

A right to choose?

Since 1935, the Voluntary Euthanasia Society (VES) (at one time called 'Exit') has campaigned to change the law. Its members believe that they should be able to choose to die if they can't face any more suffering. They believe that death is better than a life that is

What makes life worth living? Jack Clemo is a poet who is deaf and blind. His wife 'talks' to him by tracing letters onto his hand

not worth living, so they say the law should allow doctors to help incurable patients to die peacefully if they want to. They want 'the right to die with dignity'.

The patient would have to sign a form at least 1 month beforehand to make his wish clear. Two people would have to witness his signature. These people must have nothing to gain by his death. Then, at the time of death, two doctors would have to state that the patient was suffering from a painful and incurable disease before they killed him. All these rules are suggested to make sure that no one could be killed against his will.

In 1969, Lord Raglan presented a Bill to the House of Lords to legalise voluntary euthanasia. This bill was defeated, but sooner or later the subject is bound to come up again. In 1980, the VES announced that since a doctor could not legally help someone to die, it would publish a booklet *A Guide to Self-Deliverance*, telling people how they could kill themselves painlessly. This attracted many new members to the society. The booklet was published in 1981 and no doubt some people have made use of the advice it gives. For instance, in March 1983, a famous writer, Arthur Koestler, and his wife were found dead in their London flat. Arthur Koestler was a member of the VES and he had written the preface to their booklet. He was 77 years old and suffering from two incurable diseases when he killed himself. His wife was 20 years younger and in good health, but she died with him. Would it have been better if Arthur Koestler had been able to ask his doctor for a fatal dose instead of making a suicide pact with his wife?

Should the law be changed to make this possible, as Arthur Koestler himself believed? Or are there other ways to make sure that people can die without unnecessary suffering?

Pain

We all dread pain. Many people feel they would rather end their lives than suffer pain for a long time. But is this the only alternative?

In recent years doctors have carried out a great deal of research into ways of controlling pain. Some doctors claim that when dying patients are properly cared for, pain can be brought to an end.

Take Mr H., for example. When he went into a hospice he told the doctor that he had been in agony for 3 months. He had a very painful cancer. He couldn't move without great pain. It even hurt him to breathe. Once he had been given suitable pain-killing drugs he was quite changed. 'Two days after coming to the hospice he was sitting up, relaxed and smiling,' reports the doctor.

This doctor claims that many of his patients never feel pain again. Many of them are able to return home, so long as they keep on taking their pain-killers. He carried out a survey of a thousand patients nearing death, who were cared for by the staff of the hospice while they lived at home. Ninety-five per cent of them had little or no pain. With the right drugs pain can be controlled and the patient remains clear-headed.

A worthwhile life?

Once the pain has gone a dying person can often live a fairly normal life until the end. He can see friends and members of his family. He won't want to be left alone with only a television set for company. Although he is not likely to be able to work, he may still have plenty to give to the people around him. If they can help him see that he is a valuable person and his life is worth living, will he still want it to be brought to an end?

Kill or care?

> 'I'm sorry you're in pain and lonely. You don't have much to live for any more, do you? Perhaps you'd like to take this pill. Soon you won't feel a thing...'

This imaginary doctor may have a soothing bedside manner, but his prescription would be fatal. Is death the only comfort we can offer to those who are weak and ill, nearing the end of their lives? One doctor tells this story:

> 'A very unhappy old lady called Mrs E. came to our clinic at the hospice one Thursday. Her husband had just died. The grief had caused a flare-up of her arthritis. She was much weakened by a cancer. In tears she complained that life was not worth living. She didn't want to go on. Couldn't I just finish her off please—that euthanasia thing she's seen them talking about on telly?

"You mean you want me to kill you?" I asked.
"Yes I do."
"Well, all right then," I said reluctantly. "There's no one would know. Only me and the nurse—and she won't say anything, will you, Sister? (Sister shot me an anxious look.) We'll do it now, love, with an injection. Hold your arm out. Sister, pass me a syringe—no, not that. The big one. We'll need a lot to be sure to kill her. Come on, Mrs E.—hold your arm out."
But the arm was behind her back. She gave me a nervous giggle ... Then Mrs E. said something which I will never forget: "No, doctor. What I mean is ... aren't you going to do something to help me?"'

If a young person tries to commit suicide it is very often a cry for help. If an old, sick person asks for mercy-killing, might it be the same cry?

Can we afford to care?

At the moment many people who are old and frail live in very bad conditions. Every winter there are stories in the newspapers about old people dying alone in cold, damp rooms. Some families have to bear the whole burden of caring for an elderly relative who is ill and very demanding. They may get very little help from anyone else. Old people's homes are overcrowded and good nursing homes are very expensive. The care that hospices give uses a lot of staff and it costs money to employ them. Can we afford to give proper care to people nearing the end of their lives?

Some people who are in favour of mercy-killing look at it from the point of view of cost. The VES says its members are 'eager to see the best possible doctoring and nursing always available for all who need and want such care'. But the organisation goes on to say that because money is always short, members don't want it to be wasted on taking care of people 'who definitely want to die'.

This sounds fair enough—but would it stop there? Once it became legal to choose death would we still try to care? Would people who are old and sick be made to feel it was their duty to die? 'Come on now, Mrs Smith, you don't want to be a burden on your daughter, do you? Just sign this form...'

One doctor has said, 'I can see the state taking over and insisting on euthanasia.' Care for the old and sick costs a lot of money. Much of it comes from our taxes. It could be much cheaper to give a 'death pill' and do away with the problem.

A warning from the past

Before the Second World War, one type of mercy-killing was being planned on a large scale in Germany. Hitler ordered all state hospitals and homes for the sick 'to report on patients who had been ill for 5 years or more or who were unable to work'. These reports were used to choose people for what was called mercy-killing. Yet no one consulted the patients who were to be killed, or their relatives. After the death, relatives were sent a letter which stated: 'In view of the nature of his serious, incurable ailment, his death

… is to be regarded merely as a release.' The family members were also asked to meet the costs arising from their relative's death.

A mercy? For whom?

People who want to introduce voluntary euthanasia today certainly don't want to see anything like the programme that was carried out in Nazi Germany. That was not 'death with dignity'. But is their campaign pushing us in that direction? Once we see killing as a cheaper alternative to caring could we be taking the first step along that road?

What does 'the right to die with dignity' really mean? Can a good death be guaranteed by making voluntary euthanasia legal? Might a higher standard of care for the dying be a better solution?

Three years after Lord Raglan proposed his Euthanasia Bill to the House of Lords, he announced that he had changed his mind. He now felt that euthanasia would not be needed if care for the dying was brought up to the standard he had seen in hospices.

Difficult decisions

Whatever the law says, there are still difficult decisions to be made. Doctors, their patients and the patients' relatives may all have to be involved in making them.

'Is Mr Jones responding to treatment or not? Will a new type of therapy just give him more pain? Should treatment be stopped so that the disease can take its course? How can we make him comfortable until the end?'

'What should happen to Gran now that she can't look after herself any more? Can anything be done about her painful arthritis? Do we have room for her to come and live with us? Could she stand the noise the children make?'

'What do I want to happen to me when I get old and sick? What makes life worth living for me?'

Medical advances have done much to help us. As a result many more of us are living into old age. But we can't live for ever. What should happen at the end?

8

A life worth living?

'If a child were not declared alive until 3 days after birth, then all parents could be allowed the choice only a few are given under the present system. The doctor could allow the child to die if the parents so chose and save a lot of misery and suffering.'

Dr James D. Watson, Nobel Prize Winner

'No family has ever asked, "Why did you work so hard to save the life of my child?" No grown child or young adult has ever asked, "Why did you struggle so hard when you knew the outcome would not be perfect?"'

Dr Everett Koop, Surgeon General of the USA

For most of us, incurable illness or handicap only strike after we've had many years of active life. But when a baby is born with a severe handicap the question of mercy-killing can come up right at the start of life. Should a severely handicapped baby be allowed to die?

When we think about this problem we need to work out our opinions on points like these:

- If a baby is severely handicapped does that mean that his life won't be worth living?
- How much say should parents have in what happens to their baby?
- Should doctors struggle to save the life of every baby?
- If a handicapped baby is not fed or kept warm, is he being killed, or is he just being allowed to die?

The information in the next two chapters may help you to work out what you think.

9

'There's something wrong with your baby...'

These are words that every parent dreads. A new baby should bring happiness to his parents and congratulations from their friends. When a baby's born with a handicap the smiles turn to tears. It's a terrible shock.

Some problems found at birth can quickly be put right by an operation or other treatment, but others will cause serious handicap throughout a person's life. Some of these develop long before a baby is born.

If something goes wrong in the first 3 months of pregnancy, the growing baby will probably be harmed. German measles, for instance, can cause a baby to be born handicapped. If a woman catches German measles in early pregnancy it can lead to heart defects and deafness in her baby. Girls can now be vaccinated to protect them against German measles before they start having children.

Some drugs taken in early pregnancy are harmful. Thalidomide was one. Women who took it to stop morning sickness had handicapped babies. After many years they won some compensation for their children.

Does it run in the family?

Some parents are more likely to have handicapped babies than others because of illnesses that run in the family. In some families there's a particular risk of something going wrong with the spine, causing 'spina bifida' (cleft spine). In severe cases this can mean that the person affected won't be able to walk and he'll have no control over his bladder or bowels. He may also suffer from brain damage.

Most couples run very little risk of having a baby who suffers from spina bifida—the risk is about 1 in 300. But if a close relative already has it the risk can be much greater. Couples who are at risk can take advice from their doctor. Then they can decide for themselves whether to have children or not, and work out how they could cope if they were to have a handicapped child.

Through no fault of their own...

Other handicaps can come quite out of the blue. For example, Down's syndrome (mongolism) is caused when something goes wrong right at the beginning, when the baby is conceived.

Each cell of the human body is made up of 46 chromosomes, arranged in 23 pairs. People with Down's syndrome have one extra chromosome in each cell. This tiny defect changes their appearance, harms their general health and damages their brains.

'Nina'—a girl born with Down's syndrome who has appeared in the TV programme *Crossroads*

Sometimes the effects are serious, but in other cases they are fairly mild. It's quite difficult to tell, when a baby's born with Down's syndrome, how he'll develop as he grows up.

Usually Down's syndrome doesn't run in the family, but the risks of a baby being born with it do increase with the mother's age. It's very rare for a girl of 20 to give birth to a Down's baby, but a woman over 40 runs a much greater risk.

A difficult birth

Other forms of mental handicap can be caused during the birth itself. If the birth takes a long time the baby may go short of oxygen, which is vital to life. If this happens the baby's brain will be affected before anything else.

In the past, brain damage at birth was a common cause of mental handicap. Today most hospitals use machines to keep a careful check on the baby while he's being born if there's any chance that problems may arise. If the baby's heartbeat starts to slow down this shows up on the machine, and the midwife will act quickly to prevent him being harmed.

Prevention is better than cure

As medical knowledge increases, more types of abnormality in newborn babies can be prevented.

Any woman who's expecting a baby is encouraged to attend a clinic and to see her doctor regularly. He will check that she's not putting on too much weight or developing high blood pressure, which could damage her own health and the health of her baby. She'll be warned not to smoke or drink too much and she'll be advised about what to eat. All these things help to make sure that as many babies as possible are born normal and healthy.

Abortion and the handicapped baby

It's now possible to detect some forms of handicap before a baby's born, by taking a small amount of liquid from the womb and testing it. This test (known as amniocentesis) can't be done till after the sixteenth week of pregnancy. It is often offered to women who already have a handicapped child.

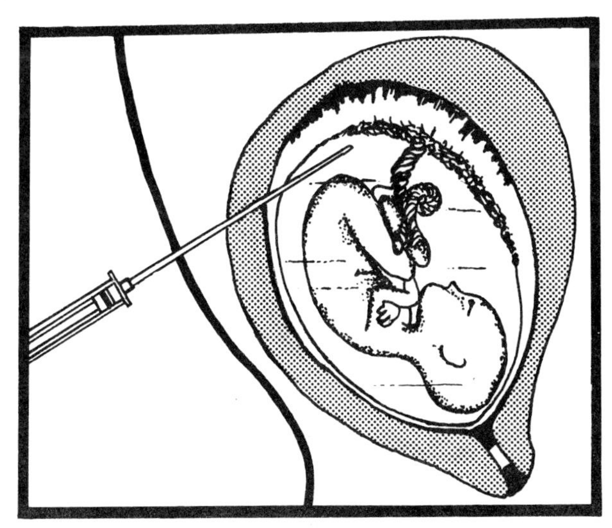

Pre-natal screening

Both spina bifida and Down's syndrome can be detected like this. If one of them is suspected, the woman has a difficult decision to make. Should she continue with her pregnancy and risk giving birth to a handicapped baby, or should she accept the offer of an abortion? In 1981, over 2,000 such women decided to have an abortion. But this pre-birth test cannot show how severe any handicap will be, and if a woman has felt her baby moving, she probably feels very attached to him. What is she to do?

If you found out that you might be the parent of a handicapped child, how do you think you would react? What sorts of things would affect your decision? There are no easy answers.

Choices at birth

What should happen when a severely handicapped baby is born? If a doctor can carry out an abortion on a pregnant woman whose baby may be handicapped, should he also be allowed to withhold treatment from a handicapped baby? Should the baby be 'allowed to die'?

These difficult problems hit the headlines in 1981, when two court cases were in the news. Both cases concerned babies born with Down's syndrome.

Baby John Pearson was born in Derby in June 1980. When his parents found out he was handicapped, they felt they couldn't cope. Dr Leonard Arthur, who was in charge of the case, prescribed 'nursing care only' for baby John. This meant that the baby wouldn't be fed. He was given only water to drink and doses of sedative. Three days after his birth, John Pearson died.

Dr Arthur was taken to court, accused of attempting to murder baby John. After a long and complicated trial he was found not guilty.

Baby Alexandra was born in London in August 1981. As well as suffering from Down's syndrome she had a blocked intestine. This problem can usually be corrected by a simple operation, but without the operation Alexandra would have died. Alexandra's parents refused to agree to the operation because they knew she was handicapped.

A social worker stepped in and baby Alexandra was made a ward of court. A judge ruled that baby Alexandra should have her operation. The operation was successful and Alexandra has progressed well. When she left hospital she went to a foster home and 4 months later she was adopted.

Who decides?

Who should decide what will happen when a handicapped baby is born? In the next chapter we'll see what choices there are and how they affect the people who have to make them—doctors, nurses and parents—as well as the baby who's on the receiving end.

10

Who decides?

Do handicapped children have a right to life? Or, if a baby's born badly handicapped, should he have a right to die? These are the questions that lie behind three different ways of caring for badly handicapped newborn babies that are used today. A handicapped baby may be given normal food and care and as much treatment as possible. At the other extreme he may be drugged, not fed, and allowed to die. A third way is to give food and normal care, but no special treatment. Let's look at what happens when each of these methods is followed.

1 Food, care and treatment

Some parents are determined that everything should be done to save their baby, even if he's very badly handicapped. Some doctors believe that all children have a right to live, so they will do everything they can to save the life of every baby in their care.

When babies are born with spina bifida, many kinds of operations can be done to try to help them. The results can be very different, as these examples show:

When **Peter** was 6 he couldn't walk, but he could get about on a 'trolley' until he was old enough to have a wheelchair. He did errands for his mother and played with other children.

Margaret, at 6, could walk normally and she went to the local village school. She was very intelligent and doing well, but she had no control over her bladder or bowels, so she had to wear nappies all the time.

Joan died at the age of 3 in spite of all the operations she'd had. She was in and out of hospital all her life. Looking back, her mother said, 'I'm grateful to have had her for 3 years as she brought a lot of love into the family, especially to me.' But she also felt she could never go through a time like that again, and she was too frightened to risk having another baby.

In recent years doctors have tried to work out which spina bifida babies will make good progress after treatment, and which are likely to remain badly handicapped. Now some doctors will advise parents that certain babies should be allowed to die.

2 No food or treatment

Both doctors and parents are involved in the decision to allow a handicapped baby to die. One doctor thinks about it like this: 'What would I answer if the child when he came of age should ask me, "Why did you let me live?"' This doctor believes that if parents care enough about their child to love and support him in spite of his handicap, the child may have a worthwhile life. But if parents have any doubts, or reject their baby, he can offer them a way out.

The way out is not to give the baby any food—just a

sedative, so that he won't cry for food. Without food any baby will die, but a hungry baby usually cries and this reminds the person who's caring for him that he needs milk. If a baby's sedated he won't cry, but he'll gradually grow weaker.

A doctor may only be involved at the start of a case like this, but nurses have to care for the baby while he's dying. They have to watch him get worse, knowing they can do nothing about it. The first effect of the sedative on baby John Pearson was to make it difficult for him to breathe, and he turned grey. Later he began vomiting. The next day he started whimpering and began to have muscle spasms before he finally died.

But what about the parents? They've suffered the shock of finding out that the new baby they've been looking forward to is handicapped. They may be asking, 'Why has this happened to us?' They may be longing for a way out. If a doctor can offer a 'solution' by allowing the child to die, they may see this as the answer to their prayers. But when parents are given some help—and hope—their feelings can change.

Mary Craig already had three children when her son Nicholas was born. One of them, Paul, was handicapped. Paul suffered from a rare disease and he was very difficult to care for. He couldn't talk and he didn't even seem to recognise his mother. When Nicholas was born Mary thought she'd come to terms with this tragedy, and she was looking forward to the arrival of her new baby.

Then Mary discovered that Nicholas suffered from Down's syndrome. The doctor told her a few hours after he was born. Half an hour later, Mary heard there were complications and Nicholas was rushed off to another hospital for an emergency operation. At that point Mary hoped that her baby would die:

> 'At this stage, Nicholas was no more than an unfortunate happening, and now there was a distinct hope that the misfortune might be blotted out. God, how I wanted that to happen.'

But Nicholas came through the operation, and when Mary took him home, her feelings suddenly changed. He became part of the family at once.

> 'Something happened to all of us that first evening; we all became his devoted slaves. Perhaps it was his helplessness, I don't know. What I do know is that I loved him before that first evening was out, we loved him, and there was no more wishing that he would die. From then on the struggle was to keep him alive.'

3 Food and care, but no special treatment

Many doctors don't agree with those who said at Dr Arthur's trial that a handicapped baby may be starved and sedated to speed his death. They believe that all newborn babies should be fed and cared for, whether or not they're handicapped. In May 1983, the British Medical Association issued new guidelines to doctors. Among other things, these said that all babies should be given milk.

This form of care could give seriously handicapped babies a chance to fight back. Some of them do just that. In March 1982, a newspaper report gave two examples.

One woman's baby was born severely handicapped. The doctors said it wasn't worth treating her. But when she was 2 she was walking, talking and feeding herself. She would soon be starting nursery school.

Another mother had a 4-year-old girl with spina bifida. She'd had no special operations because the doctors hadn't thought she would live, but she'd turned out to be a very intelligent, happy child.

These children had done well with food and normal care.

A change in the law?

At present the law says that any doctor who deliberately ends his patient's life, whether that patient is old or young, is a murderer. After Dr Arthur was found not guilty of attempted murder, the Director of Public Prosecutions (DPP) said, 'I don't want to be put into the position again of regarding any doctor as a murderer like those we see every day in our courts ... The more that medical science advances, the more difficult it is going to become. It is not a problem which is going to disappear.'

So what should be done? Some people believe that parents should be able to choose whether their handicapped baby should live or die. A group called Prospect was set up in 1981 to campaign for this. It has had letters from parents of handicapped children who feel their lives have been wasted. One letter came from a woman of 88 who was still caring for her spastic daughter aged 66. A spokesman for Prospect said, 'The mother feels that she would have had other children had she not been compelled to accept the burden. The daughter, utterly dependent on her mother, lives in dread of the future...'

Prospect sent a draft Bill to MPs suggesting a way to change the law to allow doctors not to give treatment to handicapped newborn babies, and to take steps to end their lives. The Bill suggested that doctors should be allowed to do this in the case of handicapped babies up to 28 days old.

Other people have taken a different view.

In August 1981, Mencap (Royal Society for Mentally Handicapped Children) asked MPs to support an amendment to the Education Bill. It wanted to make sure that all parents of handicapped babies would be given advice and practical help as soon as their babies were born. The amendment gained a lot of support but it did not become law.

Today, when a baby is born with Down's syndrome his parents can be helped straightaway by the Down's Children's Association (DCA). New parents can meet others who've been through the same experience and survived the shock. They can see older children who have made great strides in spite of their handicap. They can learn how to make the most of their child's abilities and help him to live a worthwhile life. Many things can be done to help Down's babies right from the start. Extra vitamins and special exercises may make a lot of difference. Once parents know how they can help their child, the future may look less bleak and they can have something to aim for.

Members of the DCA were upset when doctors who gave evidence at the trial of Dr Arthur painted such a gloomy picture of the life lived by Down's children. They felt it put back the clock 30 years and ignored all the progress they've made in helping these children.

Other organisations have been finding families to foster and adopt handicapped children, so that those who have been rejected by their own parents don't have to spend their lives in hospitals or children's homes.

One young man with Down's syndrome has published a book. *The World of Nigel Hunt* is his account of events in his life. He has written about the pop music he likes and the holidays abroad he has had with his parents. He typed the book himself. There's no doubt that Nigel, and his parents, feel his life is worthwhile.

A girl born with Down's syndrome has gained the Duke of Edinburgh's Gold Award. In January 1985, Cathy Hebden, aged 23, was presented with her award after 4 years' hard work. She had learned to swim and to do dress making. She led an expedition in Epping Forest, using a map to plan the route. She also spent time helping handicapped children. She was the first person with Down's syndrome to gain this award.

So which is the more loving course to take? Should severely handicapped babies be allowed to die, or can parents be helped to make the most of life with their handicapped child? Who can say whether his or her life will be worth living?

Hope for the future

Today cures have been found for many serious diseases. Could cures even be found for diseases that attack babies before they're born?

Some doctors are now claiming a breakthrough in preventing spina bifida. They've given extra doses of vitamins to mothers who run a high risk of giving birth to a spina bifida baby. They claim that when these vitamins are given very early in pregnancy, the baby's development is normal. If this proves to be true, many cases of spina bifida could be prevented.

There's no easy answer to the problem of Down's syndrome at present, but research is still going on. A leading specialist in this field is Professor Lejeune, who works in Paris. He believes a cure will be found. In his own words, 'Victory against Down's syndrome may not be too far off, if only the disease is attacked, not the babies.'

11

Which way forward?

In this book we've seen how life and death decisions have become part of today's world. Doctors, and their patients, have to make these decisions more and more often. Can it ever be right to end someone's life? Should the law allow it?

Many groups have called for changes in the law. Some claim a right to life. Others want a right to die. Which way will we go in the future? And which way **should** we go?

The answers we give will depend on many things, but two of the most important are these:

- What **we** think makes life worth living.
- How much we're prepared to do to make sure that as many people as possible can have lives that **they** feel are worth living.

Health and happiness

'I think the most important thing for anyone is health and happiness. As long as I'm healthy I'll be quite happy.'

Jackie

'I really think that all my operations and all the things I had wrong with me were worth it, because I really enjoy life and I don't really let the things that are wrong with me bother me...'

A seriously handicapped young man

Most of us feel, like Jackie, that our health is very important to our happiness. Perhaps we feel that if we lost our health, life would no longer be worth living.

Who can say what makes life worth living? Can one person judge this for another? A doctor who's an expert on kidney disease recently said on the radio that he'd rather die than spend his life depending on a kidney machine. A few days later, a kidney patient replied, saying that she's grateful for the extra years of life the machine has given her. She's got used to using the machine for many hours each week, and she no longer expects to be able to do all the things she used to do. She's pleased to be alive at all.

An independent life?

Ann Gray works as a shorthand typist. She lives in her own flat and drives her own car. She's engaged to be married. None of these things is very unusual, but Ann is quite an unusual person. She was born with severe spina bifida and she can't walk. She's had to have one leg amputated and she can't control her bladder. How does she manage to lead an independent life?

John Howick setting off for work in his specially adapted car. John was born with spina bifida

'Really it's all quite simple if you work it out beforehand. I get myself breakfast at 6.45 a.m. ... I get myself into the bath by easing myself from my chair onto a stool and then into the bath ... at 7.50 I start making my way out of the flats to drive myself to work in my 'Trike'. Work starts at 8.30 a.m. The canteen where I have lunch is on the same floor as my office, so I am lucky there ... At 5.30 I drive myself home. The first thing I do when I get home is to make myself a cup of tea ...'

Ann also goes on camping holidays specially organised for handicapped people, which she enjoys very much.

Does Ann live a worthwhile life? Certainly she faces problems, but many of them are caused by able-bodied people who don't try to understand how she feels. For example, she says, 'Please, please, don't talk through us, at us, or around us. Sometimes one able-bodied person will call to another one in my presence and say, "Does she want a cup of tea?" I find this quite maddening.'

Have you ever done that?

The world about us

It's not only our attitudes that can prevent disabled people from living a full life. Buildings are often designed with no thought for handicapped users.

Since 1970, council grants have been available to help handicapped people to live in their own homes. One person may need a chair lift to get him upstairs.

Another might have to use a special hoist to get in and out of bed. Aids like this can be very expensive and many people can't afford them. A grant can help a lot.

Changes to public buildings cost money too. Do you study at a college or further education centre? How easy is it for someone in a wheelchair to get to the room where your class is held? Are there too many stairs, or awkward corners to turn? What changes would have to be made to make it possible for him or her to join your group?

Local councils don't always spend money on things like this, although by law they have to make sure that disabled people can get into public buildings.

Special care

It's even more expensive to provide special homes to care for people who are very severely handicapped. Homes for old people and people who are dying also cost a lot to run. Too often in the past we've tried to cope with these problems without spending much money. Handicapped people and old people have spent their days in dreary hospital wards where they just go downhill. When the National Health Service has to cut back its spending, care for old people and handicapped people usually suffers. Charities have often shown the way ahead in providing special care.

The Cheshire Homes are famous for the care they give to young disabled people. The first of these homes, 'Le Court', in Hampshire, now has a workshop

John Evans has been paralysed from the neck down and in all four limbs since he broke his neck in 1975. He lived at the 'Le Court' Cheshire Home for 5 years. Amongst other things he is now chairman of Project '81, which helps residents of homes to move out and live in the community if they want to. He has travelled to the USA and is now studying with the Open University

where disabled residents can do photography, printing and watch repairing. They also publish their own monthly newspaper and take a full part in running the Home. For example, they help to interview new staff.

There are now over 60 Cheshire Homes in Britain and even more abroad, in Africa, India and the Far East as well as Europe and America.

For many young people a stay in a Cheshire Home may be a step towards a more independent life. One person may find a job, or another might decide to get married, so they move out. But their stay in the Home has given them the confidence they needed to branch out and fend for themselves.

Homes for people who are old and weak, and for people with fatal illnesses, are often run by charities. Most hospices were started by charities too. All these organisations depend on our generosity for their support.

Give and take

Many disabled people can give a lot to others. Some severely handicapped people are able to work from the homes where they live so that they're earning something towards their keep.

Richard is a freelance computer programmer. He was born a spastic. He's also partly deaf and he finds it hard to speak clearly. Richard couldn't go to school, but his mother taught him to read and he became very interested in mathematics and science.

Richard has learnt to use a special typewriter which he controls by a foot pedal instead of using his fingers. Now he lives in a home run by the Spastics' Society. He's taken a university course in computer programming and does freelance work.

Eunice suffers from spina bifida. For years she lived in a hospital where she had to spend most of her time in bed. At last a social worker found her a place in a residential workshop where she could lead a more active life.

At the workshop Eunice paints patterns on ceramic tiles. She's paid the proper rate for the job. She has her own room in the hostel and she pays rent out of her wages. Eunice now has an electric car, so she can get out for local trips, and she's been able to afford a couple of holidays—she's flown to Jersey and to the Hebrides.

Old and young

Old people, too, may have a lot to give. Every year the number of retired people in this country grows. They need all sorts of services that young people usually don't need, such as meals on wheels and home helps. They go to see their doctors more often and they need more prescriptions. Do they just use up taxpayers money or can they give something in return?

The most important thing that elderly people have is

time, and that's something that the rest of us often lack. A TV programme about old people showed a woman in her eighties visiting a young spastic man and helping him to 'talk' using a special sign board. She said that she thought he'd prefer a younger visitor, but she had the time to go to see him, while younger people didn't.

The price of life

When we add up the cost of caring for people who are handicapped, old or sick, what should we take into account? Is it just a matter of pounds and pence? When your taxes are being spent to provide such care, do you resent it?

Or do we gain in any way if we try to make sure that people who have special needs get every possible chance to enjoy life? The time may come when we need such help ourselves. How will we feel about the costs then?

They say that everything has its price. What's the price of life?

Acknowledgements

The author and publishers are grateful for permission to quote information and statistics and to reproduce copyright material as follows:

Chapter 3
Quote from 'Sally' taken from *The Ambivalence of Abortion* by Linda Bird Francke (Penguin, 1980)
Abortion figures for 1981 from *Abortion Statistics* (HMSO)
Quote from 'Maggy' from *Mixed Feelings* (Women's Reproductive Rights Information Centre, 1984)

Chapter 4
Gallup poll conducted for *Brass Tacks* (BBC TV programme, 1979)
Statistics and material on late abortions from 'Human Concern' (SPUC paper, winter 1979) and a report by the Royal College of Obstetricians and Gynaecologists (1984)
Case of NHS delays from *Why Late Abortion?* (Birth Control Campaign, 1980)
Figures on children in care in Britain from *Social Trends* (HMSO)
Details of Life houses from *Life News* (autumn 1983)

Chapter 6
Figures on where people die from *Care of the Dying* by Dr Richard Lamerton (Pelican Books, revised edition, 1980). Also quotes from a hospice doctor and his patients throughout this chapter and in Chapter 7; and the case of Mrs N.
The case of Mrs Arnold reported in *The Observer* (October, 1980)
Jean's Way by Derek Humphrey and Ann Wickett (Quartet Books, 1978)
Sheila Hancock quoted in *Kill or Care* by John Searle (Paternoster Press, 1977)

Chapter 7

'One doctor' (page 48) was Dr John Goundry, quoted in *Whatever Happened to the Human Race?* by F. Schaeffer and E. Koop (Marshall, Morgan & Scott, 1980)
Details of Nazi euthanasia programme from 'Medical Science Under Dictatorship' by Leonard Alexander, *New England Journal of Medicine* 241, pp. 39–47, 14 July 1949

Chapter 8

Quotes from Schaeffer and Koop, *Whatever Happened to the Human Race?*

Chapter 10

The cases of Peter, Margaret and Joan taken from *The Treatment and Care of Spina Bifida Children* by Nancy Allen (Allen & Unwin, 1975)
One doctor's policy of non-treatment from *The Lancet* (24 November 1979)
Mary Craig's experiences from her book *Blessings* (Coronet Books, Hodder and Stoughton, 1979)
Professor Lejeune quoted from *The Lancet* (5 January 1980)

Chapter 11

Handicapped young people quoted from Schaeffer and Koop, *Whatever Happened to the Human Race?*
Ann Gray's case quoted from *The Treatment and Care of Spina Bifida Children* by Nancy Allen
The cases of Richard and Eunice from *Despite Disability* edited by R. Bleakely (Educational Explorers Ltd, 1974)

Thanks are also due to Tricia Porter, who took the photographs on pp. 6, 11, 13, 26, 32, 43, 70, 73 and 76; and to the following copyright holders for permission to reproduce illustrations: The Society for the Protection of the Unborn Child p. 19; *Nursing Mirror* p. 35; Derek Bayes p. 38; Central Independent Television Plc p. 55; Medical Educational Trust p. 57.

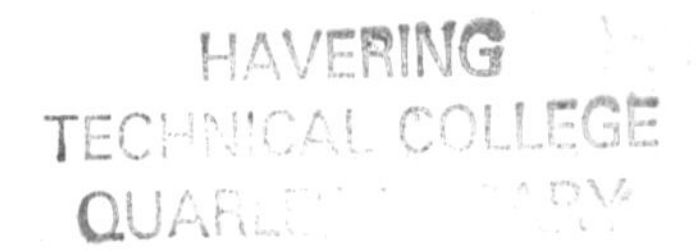